FLOWERING BULBS

DAVID JOYCE

COLLINS

Editors Maggie Daykin, Susanne Mitchell
Designer Chris Walker
Picture research Moira McIlroy

First published 1988 by
William Collins Sons & Co Ltd
London · Glasgow · Sydney
Auckland · Toronto · Johannesburg

British Library Cataloguing in Publication Data

Joyce, David
  Flowering bulbs. —— (Collins Aura garden
  handbooks).
  1. Bulbs 2. Flowers
  I. Title
  635.9'44   SB425

  ISBN 0–00–412385–9

Photoset by Bookworm Typesetting
Printed and bound in Hong Kong by Dai Nippon Printing
Company

Front cover: Lilium auratum
Back cover: Cyclamen neapolitanum
Both by Pat Brindley

CONTENTS

INTRODUCTION

In the modern garden bulbs are very important ornamental plants. Many – including some of the loveliest – are easy to grow and they range in size from giants, taller than a man, to miniatures of exquisite refinement. Some are vividly coloured while others are of a quiet, subtle beauty, and their scents include some of the sweetest and richest among flowering plants. Also, there is a good choice of hardy species and varieties that will ensure flowers in the garden at all seasons, and indoors they provide some of the showiest and most welcome flowers in the dead of winter.

The history of bulb growing

The hundreds of species and the innumerable cultivated varieties that make up this vast repertoire of garden plants are the result of centuries of exploration, collecting and cultivation. The arrival in Vienna, and later the Netherlands, towards the end of the sixteenth century, of bulbs or their seeds from Turkey, was a development of great significance. It marked the beginning of the commercially important tradition of bulb growing in the Netherlands and in the 1630s led to the wild speculation in tulip varieties. The documented evidence available before the sixteenth century is rather fragmentary but it is clear that bulbs such as lilies and crocuses were cultivated in the ancient world and the tradition survived in monastic gardens until the Renaissance.

Since the early introductions of bulbs from Turkey, the bulb-rich areas of the Mediterranean and Asia Minor have been a rich source of garden plants. But other countries, too, have made major contributions to the range of bulbs we grow. The extraordinarily rich flora of South Africa, for example, gave us the gladiolus species from which modern varieties have been developed. China and Japan have contributed some of the most valued lily species, among other plants, and the widely varying climatic regions of North America have produced plants of distinctive character, of which the erythroniums are certainly some of the loveliest.

The selection of good forms, and hybridizing species to get larger and more colourful flowers, has been carried out by many hundreds of professional and amateur botanists, nurserymen and gardeners. Consequently, it is the good fortune of the modern gardener to have many fine cultivated forms as well as the species to choose from.

Gladioli, like these large-flowered hybrids which make a marvellous.show of colour in summer, grow from storage organs known as corms. Corms look rather like bulbs and are indeed treated in the same way by gardeners.

LEFT Daffodils, which are so popular for spring colour, are among the many ornamental plants that are true bulbs. The bulb is a storage organ.

BELOW LEFT *Crinum powellii* is one of the larger bulbs and although not too well-known is nevertheless fairly easy to grow given the right conditions.

What is a bulb?

The word 'bulb' loosely covers a wide range of plants which all have underground organs for storing food. The typical annual cycle of these plants consists of a period of growth, generally during a wet season, when the plants use the food stored in the bulb, and is followed by flower and then seed production. The growth period is followed by a period of rest, during which the leaves of many bulbs will die down and the plant becomes dormant once more.

Daffodils, hyacinths, lilies and tulips are among the many ornamentals that are true bulbs. In these plants the bulb consists of tightly folded scales springing from a base plate. The scales are modified leaves which are the plant's food store. When the plant is in growth it feeds off the food stored in the scales and the bulb therefore diminishes in size. When active growth is at an end a reverse process returns food from the above ground part for storage in the next season's bulb scales. Because of this reverse process it is important that the leaves of bulbs should not be cut after flowering; allow them to die down naturally.

Although superficially looking like true bulbs, the storage organs of a number of plants – among them crocuses, freesias and gladioli – are correctly known as corms. Generally covered by a papery skin, they are rather flat, rounded shapes and are the swollen bases of stems. After flowering, the corms shrivel but are replaced by new ones formed in the growing season.

Tubers, either formed from swollen roots, as is probably the case with species of *Cyclamen*, or from modified underground stems (rhizomes) as in the case of the wood anemone, have no base plate and the tough skins do not have a papery tunic. Some tuberous-rooted plants are commonly included in the general category of bulbs, while others – such as the dahlia – are listed with the herbaceous perennials.

PLANTING BULBS OUTSIDE

Almost all bulbs, whether they are sun-loving or shade tolerant, need well-drained soil. If the soil in your garden is naturally heavy and sticky it can be lightened by the addition of sand and peat.

The regal lily, *Lilium regale*, is an easy plant, worth a place in any collection of bulbs. The richly scented flowers are produced in clusters in mid-summer, on stems up to about 1.8m (6ft) high.

Some of the lightest soils are not sufficiently moisture retentive for some woodland bulbs. Lilies and erythroniums, for example, must not have stagnant conditions but do need a plentiful supply of moisture. Light soils can be improved to some extent by adding organic material such as leafmould, peat or 'Forest Bark' Ground and Composted. Modifying your garden soil to suit the plants you want to grow can only be partially effective. You will achieve the best results by growing plants that suit the existing soil conditions.

It is very important that if you add to the soil organic matter in the form of manure or compost, this should be thoroughly decomposed; fresh manure should never come into contact with bulbs. A bed that has been dug and had compost added should be allowed to settle for a week or two before bulbs are planted. Bulbs that particularly benefit from a high humus or organic content in the soil include gladioli, hyacinths used in bedding schemes and lilies.

Relatively few bulbs are lime- or chalk-haters. Some lilies need lime-free soil but others will tolerate a wide range of soils. Some bulbs, including daffodils, hyacinths and irises, do particularly well on chalk.

When to plant

To get the best results, bulbs must be planted in their appropriate season. For most bulbs this is when they are dormant but some, such as snowdrops, do better if they are planted after flowering but before the leaves have died down.

The classic bulbs of spring, including daffodils, tulips and the many early-flowering small bulbs, are planted in late summer or early autumn. In the case of most of these, the earlier they are planted the better. So, if you are buying from a nurseryman, order them in good time and, if you are buying from a garden centre, purchase bulbs as soon as they come in.

In the autumn planting timetable daffodils should be given priority. They start rooting early and need ample time to do so before developing top growth. Tulips should be planted at the end of autumn. If they are planted early, there is an increased risk that they will be attacked by disease. Although lilies are essentially summer-flowering bulbs, they are best planted in the autumn but can be planted right through to early spring, provided planting is done in mild weather.

The autumn-flowering bulbs, which deserve to be much more widely grown than they are, should be planted in late summer or very early autumn; it is often rather late before they become available. The flowers can shoot up with astonishing speed – within a matter of days – after planting.

The more tender summer-flowering bulbs, such as gladioli, cannot be planted out until mid-spring. However, in order to get flowers in mid-summer, they can be started into growth in a frost-free greenhouse, then planted out in the open garden when there is little further danger of frost.

ABOVE LEFT Dutch irises, like this variety: 'Wedgwood', are easy to grow in well-drained soil and make good cut flowers.

LEFT Hyacinths can be mass planted in beds and are also ideal for containers such as tubs and windowboxes

Suitable tools for planting include a narrow-bladed trowel, dibber and ordinary hand trowel. For best effect plant the bulbs in bold groups. When planting, the base of the bulb must be in close contact with the soil. There must not be an air space below, as there is with the one near-right; water collecting there would rot the bulb.

How to plant

In the wild state, bulbs often grow at surprising depths; perhaps this has something to do with the amount of nutrients and moisture in the soil. In cultivation, the depths at which bulbs are grown depends on the nature of the soil. In a light, free-draining soil bulbs should be planted more deeply than in a heavy, sticky soil. The table given opposite for the main groups of bulbs therefore allows a range of depths. In general, the larger the bulb the more deeply it needs to be planted. Almost all the small, early spring bulbs should be planted 5–10cm (2–4in) deep, although some gardeners favour deeper planting of *Iris danfordiae* to discourage splitting of the bulbs. Planting at an adequate depth is especially important with the stem-rooting lilies, that is, those that produce roots from the stem above the bulb. Cyclamen need more shallow planting than the majority of bulbous plants; most species need no more than a light covering of soil and leafmould.

Bulbs generally look more natural when planted in clumps rather than dotted about and their colour and form make a bolder effect. However, they should not be planted so closely that they compete with one another for food and water supplies. Most of the small bulbs can be planted between 5–7.5cm (2–3in) apart but daffodil and tulip bulbs will need to be spaced about 15cm (6in) apart.

For planting in clumps, first place the bulbs on the surface of the soil to establish the dimensions of the hole then use a trowel to dig down to the necessary depth, remembering that the depth given in the table refers to the soil above the bulb. Before planting, loosen the soil in the bottom of the hole. In heavy, sticky soils it is a good idea to set bulbs on a shallow bed of sand.

When planting bulbs in grass it is

important to avoid a symmetrical arrangement. Have some bulbs grouped closely but others spread out on the periphery of the clump. A trowel can be used to make individual holes but when there is a lot of planting to do a bulb planter will make the job easier: it takes up a plug of turf and soil which can be dropped back once the bulb is planted. Another method for planting in grass is to lift back a section of turf, loosen the soil underneath, put in the bulbs then replace the turf.

PLANTING PLAN FOR MAIN BULBS

	Depth of soil above bulb		Planting time
	cm	in	
Anemones	5–10	2–4	September-October March
Colchicums	10–15	4–6	July-August
Crocuses	5–10	2–4	Autumn-flowering: July-August Spring-flowering: September-October
Cyclamen (hardy)	2.5	1	July-September
Daffodils & jonquils large small	10–15 5–10	4–6 2–4	August-September
Erythroniums	10–15	4–6	September-October
Fritillaries (crown imperial)	15–20	6–8	September-October
Gladioli	10–15	4–6	February-April
Hyacinth	10–15	4–6	October-November
Irises, dwarf	5–8	2–3½	September-October
Lilies basal rooting stem rooting	10–15 15–20	4–6 6–8	September-March
Snowdrops & snowflakes	5–10	2–4	In the green: March Dry: September-October
Tulips	10–15	4–6	October-November

WHERE TO GROW BULBS

One of the loveliest ways to grow plants is to put them in a setting like that in which they would occur naturally and to let them establish self-maintaining colonies. There are few plants for growing in this way that respond as well as bulbs. A surprising number will grow vigorously in grass and others thrive happily if planted in a woodland environment.

Daffodils are most commonly and satisfactorily naturalized in grass, the larger varieties and species competing successfully even with thick grass. The older hybrids are cheaper to buy in quantity than more recent introductions and in general they look more at home in a natural setting than those with very large trumpets and cups. The poet's narcissus *(N. poeticus)*, for instance 'Actaea', is well-suited for planting in this way. Although mixtures can produce a gay effect, they never create the impression of being a naturally occurring colony.

A lawn is not the place for this kind of planting as there is a conflict between the need for frequent cutting of the grass to maintain it in prime condition and the requirement of bulbs to have their leaves die down naturally. What is needed is a stretch of grass – at the outer edge of a lawn or in an orchard – that can be left uncut for at least six weeks after bulbs have flowered. The smaller bulbs will find the competition of thick grass too fierce but in a meadow-like setting with thin grass they can be very successful. The dwarf narcissi such as *N. bulbo-*

Some bulbs, such as this white variety of the snake's head fritillary, *Fritillaria meleagris*, need a dark background if the delicate flowers are to show up well.

RIGHT Tulips are best suited to formal beds and borders, where they can be combined with wallflowers and forget-me-nots.

BELOW Scillas are ideal for naturalizing in a meadow-like setting with thin grass.

need light but flower early enough to be planted among deciduous trees. Erythroniums, bluebells and wood anemones are all tolerant of a little more shade and *Cyclamen hederifolium* will even grow among conifers.

In borders

The herbaceous border is increasingly uncommon as a garden feature on account of the work it involves. Bulbs are not so well suited to it anyway; they do not take kindly to the heavy manuring that is necessary and they are disturbed when the ground is cultivated. However, in a mixed border where shrubs and perennials are combined many niches can be found for bulbs and they provide one of the best ways of extending the border's flowering season. Deep planting will allow some cultivation of the soil once foliage has died down with little risk of the bulbs being damaged. If bulbs are planted in clumps this will make for easier cultivation of the border as well as being more effective.

codium, snowdrops, the sturdy *Crocus tommasinianus*, glory of the snow *(Chionodoxa)* and scillas and the windflower, *Anemone blanda*, will all flourish. If the soil is moist the snake's-head fritillary *(Fritillaria meleagris)* and the summer snowflake *(Leucojum aestivum)* will naturalize satisfactorily.

Although most bulbs will not thrive in heavy shade there are many that flower early, long before most deciduous trees have come into leaf. *Anemone blanda*, chionodoxas, scillas and winter aconite *(Eranthis)*

Height and light requirements are two factors to take into account when positioning bulbs. The stately crown imperial *(Fritillaria imperialis)*, for example, is best towards the back of a border. Apart from being tall, the plant gives off a foxy smell, which some people find unpleasant. Many lilies will benefit from having their bases shaded by other plants but with their heads in full sun or dappled light.

Another point to remember when positioning bulbs is that there is generally a period when the leaves are dying down rather untidily. They should not be cut but in the mixed border can often be masked by the growth of perennials or even by a planting of annuals. Another solution is to use specially designed plant trays which are set in the ground and planted up. After flowering, the bulbs in their tray can be lifted and placed in a corner of the garden out of the way while the foliage dies down.

For bedding

The spectacular massed bedding schemes that are still a feature of many public parks call for resources the private gardener is not likely to have. However, even a small bed of spring or summer flowers can be a lovely feature. The most popular bulbs for bedding are tulips and hyacinths, but others can be used, including daffodils and for an extravagant but magnificent effect lilies, such as the ever popular regal lily *(Lilium regale)*.

The most successful plantings are achieved with bulbs of one colour but they make a more complex colour harmony when combined with other bedding plants. Many tulips, particularly pink varieties such as 'Clara Butt' or white varieties such as the lily-flowered 'White Triumphator', go well with the blue of forget-me-nots; hyacinths can look lovely with pansies. Other plants for such schemes include wallflowers and bedding daisies.

ABOVE Tulips and blue muscari or grape hyacinths, combined with pansies and wallflowers, make a long-lasting spring display in sunny beds.

LEFT This is a classic combination of tulips (parrot tulips are seen here) and myosotis or forget-me-nots.

A familiar sight in spring gardens – tulips, forget-me-nots and wallflowers. Tulips are an excellent choice for containers, too.

Rock gardens and raised beds

Dwarf bulbs are ideal for the rock garden or raised bed. They associate well with perennial and shrubby alpines which, like many bulbs, require a reasonably fertile but gritty soil that is well drained. If your soil is sticky and slow-draining, a raised bed is a particularly good way of providing the growing conditions small bulbs and alpines enjoy. Walls of stone or brick need only be 30–60 cm (1–2ft) high, and should contain a gritty soil mixture over a layer of drainage material. The raised bed has the great advantage of bringing the small bulbs closer to view. It is better not to distract from the beauty of the miniature chionodoxas, daffodils and scillas – to mention just a few of the most suitable – by planting with them the showy, highly cultivated forms of bulbs. Those that require acid soils, such as erythroniums, will do well associated with dwarf rhododendrons in a raised bed made with peat blocks.

In containers

Almost all bulbs can be grown in containers such as flower-pots and windowboxes and although some – including crocuses – may deteriorate after the first season, many will perform well when planted again in subsequent years. Container-grown bulbs are particularly valued in town gardens, where they can bring to life paved yards or brighten the outlook from a window. But even in the large garden, containers planted with bulbs can be strategically placed to close a perspective and to draw attention away from parts of the garden that are dormant or otherwise uninteresting.

When selecting bulbs, make sure that they will grow to a height appropriate to the container. Plants in windowboxes are much more exposed to wind than those grown at ground level so, for these containers, choose short-growing species and varieties. Species daffodils or short hybrids such as 'Jack Snipe', *Iris reticulata* and tulips such as 'Red Riding Hood' that are derived from *Tulipa greigii* are all suitable for this purpose. In positions that are not exposed to wind, tall-growing bulbs such as lilies can be very satisfactory grown in containers.

THE CARE OF BULBS

In the open garden, the fully hardy bulbs in particular need little special attention. In an average year it is not likely that watering will be necessary. However, a bulb's period of growth normally coincides with a predictable supply of water, either from rain or snow melt, so if conditions are exceptionally dry some watering may be necessary. Plants that may particularly need this attention are those near to walls or in windowboxes where natural rainfall may not reach them. Even after flowering a good supply of water will be necessary to compensate for these less favourable situations until the foliage begins to yellow and die down.

Feeding

Before bulbs come into growth give a light feed of bonemeal or a general fertilizer. In borders lightly rake this into the topsoil.

All bulbs will benefit from the application of a quick-acting feed such as ICI Liquid Growmore every ten days or fortnight during the growing season. Feeding in this way is especially important for container-grown plants because nutrients are quickly washed out of the soil. The use of food sticks such as 'Keri-spikes' will ensure the steady release of nutrients necessary for growth and flowering.

After flowering

In the case of the most common bulbs there is little point in saving seed and as the production of seed draws on the bulbs' food resources and may, therefore, affect future flowering, it can be worthwhile to remove faded flowers. Clearly this is impractical in extensive plantings and in any case self-sown seed will help to build up naturalized bulbs, but it is a policy worth following with, for example, members of the lily family. When deadheading, leave as much of the flower stalk and foliage as possible as these will help build up the bulb for the next season's growth.

The enthusiast who grows rare and choice bulbs is a special case. The more widely the seed of such bulbs is available the less cause for the wild populations to be depleted by collection, so seeds should be allowed time to ripen, and then be sown while they are still fresh.

If the ground is needed for other plants, bulbs used for spring bedding can be lifted immediately after flowering. Then they should be heeled in, in a spare part of the garden, until the foliage has completely died down.

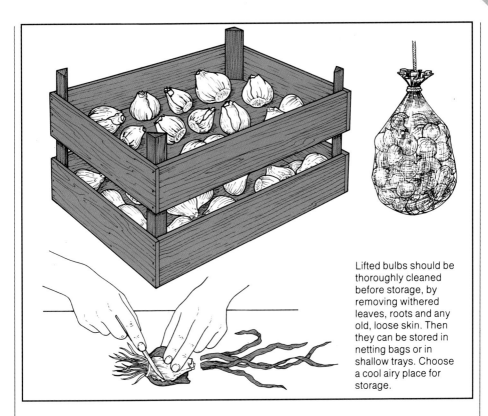

Lifted bulbs should be thoroughly cleaned before storage, by removing withered leaves, roots and any old, loose skin. Then they can be stored in netting bags or in shallow trays. Choose a cool airy place for storage.

Lifting and transplanting

Most hardy bulbs do not need to be lifted annually during their period of dormancy but the hybrid tulips are an exception. Once the foliage has died down the bulbs should be lifted and cleaned off by removing the dead foliage and any loose skins and trimming back the roots; then soak in a fungicide such as Benlate + 'Activex' before leaving them to dry and be stored where there is adequate ventilation. The more tender bulbous plants such as gladioli need to be treated in the same way and stored where there is no danger of frost damage.

Although the majority of hardy bulbs can be left in the ground from year to year, clumps can become so congested that flowering deteriorates. Therefore, any dense clumps should be lifted, divided and replanted. In general, the best time to do this is after foliage has died and the bulbs are just entering their dormant phase. However, quite a number of bulbs do not suffer from being lifted after flowering but while still in leaf and some, snowdrops and snowflakes particularly, settle down much more quickly when moved 'in the green'.

Although the leaves of many bulbs can look untidy while they die down, resist the temptation to cut them for at least six weeks after flowering; otherwise the bulbs are likely to lose strength and flowering will suffer. One final point: knotted daffodil leaves are no more attractive than leaves left loose and the practice of tying in this way may be detrimental to the bulbs.

17

THE BULB YEAR

January
In the garden, snowdrops, winter aconite and some species crocuses are in flower. Bring forced bulbs into warm rooms when flower buds are well-developed.

February
Outdoors, this is the best month for the small spring bulbs. Bring in the last of the forced bulbs. In mild weather plant lilies and, for early flowering, set gladioli to sprout in a frost-free greenhouse.

March
Daffodils at last come into their own and the first tulips are out. Complete the planting of lilies and protect any shoots from frost by covering with straw or peat. Lift and divide crowded snowdrops after flowering.

April
Tulips and hyacinths gradually take over from daffodils. Watch for pests such as aphids and slugs. Water in dry spells and deadhead large bulbs. Plant gladiolus corms outdoors.

May
Once tulips and other bulbs have finished flowering, lift and move to any spare corner of the garden if beds are needed. Watch for moulds and rots and spray against aphids. Watering may be necessary.

June
Alliums are among the first summer bulbs to flower. At the end of the month lift spring bulbs. Maintain aphid control and water gladioli. Now is the time to plant poppy anemones for autumn flowering.

This is a superb way of growing daffodils – in an area of grass, with spring-flowering shrubs such as magnolias. The grass must not be cut until the bulbs' foliage has completely died down or the bulbs will not flower so well in the following year.

Bulbs for forcing, such as hyacinths, can be planted in early autumn. Bowls and other containers should be well-crocked, that is, provided with drainage material. The tips of bulbs should be just above compost level. The pots are then placed outdoors in a frame or box and covered with peat, etc, for several weeks.

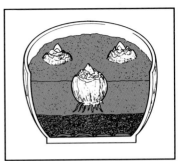
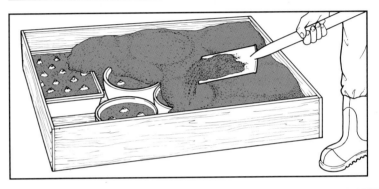

July
The first lilies come into flower. Water when necessary and spray regularly against aphids, and also thrips on gladioli. Complete the lifting and division of bulbs and begin planting autumn-flowering bulbs such as colchicums.

August
This is one of the main months for lilies and gladioli. Continue pest control and water in dry spells. Most bulb seed should be ready for sowing. Begin planting daffodils.

September
Autumn bulbs such as colchicums and cyclamen are in flower. Complete the planting of daffodils and start planting other spring bulbs (except tulips) and lilies. Bulbs for forcing must be started now.

October
Nerines make a fine display. Lift and store gladioli. Start planting tulips, complete the planting of other spring bulbs and continue planting lilies. Forced bulbs need to be checked regularly for the first signs of shooting.

November
The tender cyclamen begin to flower indoors. Complete the planting of tulips and examine forced bulbs regularly for signs of shooting. Bring bowls into a well-lit room as bulb growth develops.

December
At the end of the month the first of the forced bulbs will come into flower. Check stored gladioli and remove and destroy any that show signs of deterioration.

GROWING BULBS INSIDE

Bulbs grown indoors can be divided into three groups. Tender bulbs that require a warm environment to survive and flower; the hippeastrum is one of the most popular. Spring bulbs that are normally hardy but which are brought into flower early or forced for indoor decoration, such as specially heat-treated hyacinth and tulip bulbs. Hardy bulbs, such as species crocuses and irises, that are naturally early flowering are sometimes grown in pots or pans in a well-ventilated unheated greenhouse or frame to ensure that the flowers are not damaged by weather. This also controls more effectively than would be possible in the open garden the amount of water plants receive. If these plants are brought into the house at the moment of flowering do not place them in a very warm, centrally-heated room.

Tender bulbs

The best results with tender bulbs are generally achieved by growing them in a frost-free greenhouse and bringing them into the house at flowering time. Many home gardeners, however, have had great success with no more space than a sunny windowsill. Grow the bulbs in pots or bowls that have drainage holes, covering the holes with crocks (pieces of broken clay pots) arranged so that surplus water can drain away without the compost being washed out. Use a loam- or peat-based compost such as 'Kericompost', not the bulb fibre that is often used for forced bulbs. Plant the bulbs firmly and in the case of hippeastrum use a small pot, say 15cm (6in), with the upper half of the large bulb showing. After planting, water thoroughly and then not again until growth starts. From then until flowering, water regularly and about every ten days feed with a liquid fertilizer, such as 'Kerigrow'. Remove the flowers as they go over but leave the foliage and stems and only reduce watering as the plant begins to die down. During the dormant period the bulb can be dried off.

Generally it is not necessary to repot every year, it being sufficient to take out the top layer of compost just before growth is due to begin again, replacing it with fresh compost such as 'Kericompost' which contains a slow-release fertilizer. When repotting is carried out, set aside offsets for potting up separately.

BELOW Crocuses can be forced into early flower and they look good in special crocus pots with holes in the sides.

RIGHT Hyacinths can be in flower by Christmas time, and here are teamed with a cool foil: the maidenhair fern.

Forced bulbs

For really early and reliable results it is worth buying specially prepared bulbs. In the Northern Hemisphere, if bulbs are wanted to be in flower for Christmas they need to be planted by late summer. Bulb fibre, a peaty mixture containing some charcoal and shell, can be used in bowls without drainage holes. If fibre is used it must be thoroughly dampened before bulbs are planted in it. Plant them firmly, tulips completely covered, narcissi with their noses showing and hyacinths with about half the bulb exposed. When using a compost choose a medium one and once the bulbs are planted water thoroughly.

A common mistake is to think that once bulbs have been planted they need warmth in order to flower early. In fact, bulbs need to be put in a cool, dark place so that a good root system can develop before the leaves and flowers start growing. A cupboard in a centrally-heated house will be far too warm. If you have the space, bowls of forced bulbs can be placed in a shady part of the garden and covered with peat or ashes. Alternatively, they can be placed in a box (covered with peat and a sheet of black polythene) and kept in a cool place such as an unheated shed or cellar. The root system will take about two months to develop and during this time you should check every week or so to make sure that the planting mixture has not dried out. When the shoots are about 5cm (2in) high the bowls can be brought out and placed in a cool, well-lit room. If the temperature is too high at this stage it is very likely that the flowers will not develop and open normally. After three weeks or so in a cool room the temperature can be increased to bring on flowering.

After bulbs have flowered, remove dead flowerheads and place the bowls in a well-lit, cool but frost-free room or greenhouse. If the bulbs are planted out in the open garden in mid-spring, they will generally recover and flower again in subsequent years although they will not be suitable for forcing again.

Hyacinths and some narcissi can be forced without planting in compost or fibre; simply initiate root formation by putting the base of the bulb in contact with water and keeping the roots in water. It is still possible to buy specially made hyacinth jars for this purpose. The bulbs should be started off in a cool dark place in late summer or early autumn. Only when there is a good root system and the shoots have grown about 5cm (2in) should the bulbs be brought into the light. Keep conditions cool for about three weeks before bringing the bulbs into a warm room for flowering.

PESTS AND DISEASES

By and large, bulbs are not especially vulnerable to attack from pests and disease. By planting well-grown and healthy stock in appropriate positions, which for many bulbs will mean in sun where the soil is free-draining, many problems can be avoided. Maintaining a good standard of garden hygiene will also help; pests and diseases are much more likely to attack from a base of litter and rubbish.

Thrips are sap-sucking pests and, on gladioli in particular, cause mottling and streaking of leaves and flowers. Spraying every ten days in the growing season with 'Sybol' will keep down infestations.

Diseases

The most serious problems are those caused by viruses, as there is no satisfactory chemical way of combatting them. Attacks result in untypical mottling and streaking of leaves and flowers and eventually distorted or stunted growth. Because of the seriousness of virus disease it is worth buying stock from a reputable supplier. As aphids and other sap-sucking pests transmit viruses from one plant to another, pest control will reduce the risk of disease spreading. If it is obvious that a plant is infected, lift and burn it; *do not* add it to your compost.

A number of fungus diseases also attack bulbs, sometimes first showing as moulds and leading to the collapse of the plant. These fungi often begin working while the bulbs are in store. The danger can be minimized by storing in a cool, well-ventilated place and by treating the bulbs before storage – or in the case of new stock just before planting – with a fungicide such as Benlate + 'Activex'. By the time it is evident that a growing plant is infected it is generally too late for treatment to be effective. The foliage and bulb should be lifted and burned. Also, to prevent the infection spreading, apply Benlate + 'Activex' to the soil where the affected plant was growing and dose other bulbs in the vicinity, strictly according to the instructions on the product label. Never add more 'for good measure'.

Pests

Aphids, the greenfly and blackfly that multiply with such astonishing speed in the summer months, are pests of almost all plants. They weaken their hosts by sucking sap and, as has been mentioned under Diseases, transmit viruses from one plant to another. Thrips are also sap-sucking pests which, on gladioli in particular, cause mottling and streaking of leaves and flowers. Spraying about every ten days in the growing season with an insecticide such as 'Sybol' will keep destructive infestations down.

Some grubs, particularly those of narcissus fly, burrow into planted bulbs and lay their eggs between mid-spring and early summer. Firming the soil around bulbs may give some protection as will a dusting of an insecticide such as 'Sybol' 2.

Perhaps the most damaging of all pests are slugs and snails, which are particularly active in mild, damp weather. The most effective control is achieved by laying baits for them, such as ICI Slug Pellets, which contain metaldehyde.

Mice and voles are often attracted to newly-planted bulbs and can do a surprising amount of damage. Mice will also eat bulbs in store. A good mousing cat is probably the best answer but trapping or the use of a control such as 'Ratak' or 'Mouser' are alternatives. Rabbits may also dig up bulbs but they are much more likely to eat new shoots. In early spring, flowers – particularly crocuses – are sometimes vandalized by squirrels and birds. The most effective way to discourage birds is to insert short canes or sticks into the soil to support a criss-cross of black cotton just above the plants.

ABOVE Among the most damaging of pests are snails, which are most active in mild, damp weather.

LEFT Slugs are equally damaging. Both can be controlled by laying slug pellets around groups of bulbs.

PROPAGATION

Bulbs tend to be much slower to reach flowering size when raised from seed than most herbaceous plants. This is why the ability of many bulbs to increase vegetatively, by splitting or by the formation of bulblets or cormlets, is so important. They make it possible to raise stock that is true to the parent fairly quickly. When bulbs have died down after flowering they can be lifted and the parent bulbs and large offsets sorted for planting and flowering the following season.

Small bulbs and cormlets that are to be used to increase stocks should be planted, at the season appropriate to the parent bulbs, in a shallow trench on a layer of sand. The aerial bulblets produced by some lilies at the junction of leaves and stem can be treated in the same way. After a year or two the bulbs can be lifted in the dormant period and planted out in permanent positions. In the case of tender species and varieties the offsets will need to be grown on, probably in pots, in the frost-free conditions that are required by the parent plants in order to flourish.

Bulbs such as hyacinths and scillas that naturally produce relatively few offsets can be induced to form bulblets by being cut across the base. Make the criss-cross cut to about a third of the depth of the bulb and keep it open by inserting small pebbles or crocks. Plant the cut bulb and in the second year lift it to detach the bulblets that have formed. These will have to be grown on for several years before they reach flowering size.

Lilies can be propagated in autumn or early spring by detaching scales of healthy specimens, with

  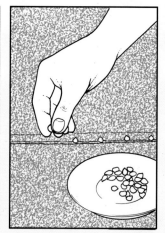

At the end of the season gladioli corms should be carefully lifted. Store in a frost-free place.

The tiny cormlets which have formed can be gently removed from the parent.

In the spring, the cormlets can be planted outside in an appropriate place to grow on.

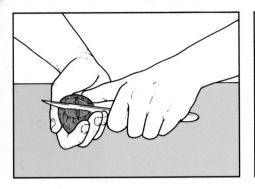
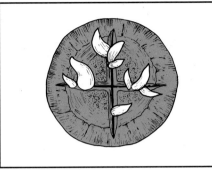

Bulbs such as hyacinths produce bulblets if they are cut across the base. Plant the cut bulb and in the second year lift it to detach the small bulblets

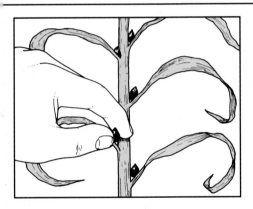

Some lilies produce bulbils in the axils of the leaves – use these for propagation. The bulbils are planted shallowly in seed trays of compost to grow on.

part of the base plate attached, and inserting these to about half their depth in seed trays containing a free-draining compost. Moderate bottom heat will help the formation of small bulbs at the base of the scales within a few months. These bulblets are best grown on in pots.

Growing from seed
The time-scale of growing bulbs to flowering size from seed may be very leisurely (some tulips may take seven years) but it is an important method for raising virus-free plants and for increasing stocks of rare species. As soon as it becomes available, seed should be sown thinly in a sandy compost in seed trays or pots. Pots can be sunk outdoors or in a frame; germination of some species may only occur after a period of cold. In the long process of raising germinated seed to mature plants you will need to keep both slugs and weeds at bay; so stay alert to them.

CHOICE BULBS

Few groups of plants are so reward-
ing as the bulbs. Most are easy to
grow and undemanding of time and
energy. They also provide a con-
tinuous source of flowers both indoors and out. The difficulty lies in
making a choice from the many
hundreds of species available, the
myriad colours, range of heights and
flower types. With this in mind, the
following list includes all the popular genera and is a handy guide to
many of the best of bulbous plants.

Allium

(Ornamental onions) As well as including some major food plants the onion family contains unusual and attractive hardy summer-flowering bulbs that are suitable for sunny positions in the rock garden or a light, well-drained border. In many species the tightly packed heads of flowers, usually borne in May/June, are suitable for cutting and can be dried for indoor decoration. One of the best of the dwarf species is *A. oreophilum (ostrowskianum)*, 10–15cm (4–6in) high, with pink or red flowers. *A. karataviense* is also short, 20cm (8in) but has huge pink flower-heads and patterned leaves. Two taller species are *A. christophii* and violet *A. rosenbachianum*, 60cm (2ft).

Amaryllis

The true amaryllis *(A. belladonna)* is an exotic and reasonably hardy plant, a native of South Africa, producing 2–4 pale pink, trumpet-shaped flowers on stems up to 75cm (2½ft) high in late summer or early autumn. The strap-shaped leaves appear after the flowers. Varieties include 'Hathor' (white) and the vigorous 'Parkeri' (deep pink).

ABOVE LEFT
Amaryllis belladonna is a reasonably hardy bulb for a sunny well-drained border.

LEFT *Allium karataviense* is ideal for a sunny rock garden or border.

ABOVE RIGHT
Anemone apennina can be naturalized under trees or in grass.

Anemone

(Dwarf species of windflower) The dwarf anemones with tuberous or rhizomatous roots include some of the best spring-flowering plants for naturalizing in grass and under trees. One of the best, *A. blanda*, has white, blue and pink forms and grows to 15cm (6in); 'Radar' is an unusual purplish-red. A very similar species is *A. apennina*. The common wood anemone, *A. nemorosa*, with up to 20cm (8in) stems, can be rampant but is an excellent choice for growing under trees.

POPPY ANEMONE HYBRIDS developed from *A. coronaria, A. pavonina* and other species, and widely grown in the flower trade, can be planted in succession to give a long-flowering summer display in borders or to provide material for cutting. The colours are mainly shades of red and blue or white and the stems are about 30cm (1ft) tall. The De Caen strain is single-flowered; the St Bavo and St Brigid strains have double or semi-double flowers.

Chionodoxa

(Glory of the snow) These very early spring bulbs are good rock-garden plants and can be naturalized with other small bulbs in thin grass. The most commonly grown species is *C. luciliae*, which produces stems up to 20cm (8in) high, carrying as many as ten blue flowers. There are in addition white and pink forms, including 'Pink Giant'. Two other species are *C. gigantea* (gentian-blue flowers) and *C. sardensis* (pale blue with a white centre).

Colchicum speciosum **is the best of the autumn crocuses.**

Colchicum

(Autumn crocus) The flowers of the autumn crocuses, not true crocuses at all, suddenly emerge at the end of summer before any sign of leaves. They are plants for a sunny position, either naturalized in grass or in borders. The best garden species, *C. speciosum*, with flowers up to 10cm (4in) long, has a fine white form as well as variations from pink to reddish-purple. *C. bornmuelleri* is similar, with paler flowers and greenish tubes. Named hybrids include 'Lilac Wonder', 'The Giant', one of the best for naturalizing in grass, and the double 'Water Lily'.

Crinum

Most of the crinums are tropical or subtropical plants but one hybrid, *C. × powellii*, is a handsome and reasonably hardy plant producing heads of lily-like flowers in late summer. The colour range is white to rose pink and the stems are up to 90cm (3ft) high. The large bulbs should be planted in a sunny position and then left undisturbed.

Crocosmia

(Montbretia) In late summer and autumn the montbretia hybrids *(C. × crocosmiiflora)* produce fans of flowers in shades of red and orange on stems about 90cm (3ft) high. In a sunny, well-drained position they will quickly build up to sizeable clumps. They are excellent and long-lasting cut flowers. Good varieties include: 'Emily McKenzie', orange with mahogany and yellow markings; 'Lucifer', flame red; and 'Vulcan', burnt orange-red.

Crocus

AUTUMN FLOWERING CROCUS SPECIES
By careful selection of species it is possible to have crocuses in flower from early autumn to mid-spring. The outstanding autumn-flowering species is *C. speciosus*, very easy to grow and ideal for naturalizing. The flowers, up to 10cm (4in) high, in varying intensities of blue, appear before the leaves. 'Aitchisonii' is the largest form and 'Oxonian' has the deepest colouring. Another autumn-flowering species is *C. kotschyanus* (*C. zonatus*).

VARIETIES OF *C. chrysanthus* The forms of *C. chrysanthus* are the loveliest of the winter or early spring crocuses. The flowers, in blue, yellow or white, are often beautifully marked or feathered. The following are representative of the many named varieties: 'Blue Bird', purplish-blue and white; 'Cream Beauty', creamy yellow; 'Lady Killer', white with mauve markings; 'Zwanenburg Bronze', orange heavily marked with purplish-brown.

LATE WINTER OR EARLY SPRING FLOWERING CROCUS SPECIES In addition to the large number of crocuses derived from *C. chrysanthus* (see preceding entry) there are a number of species that come into flower in the coldest months of the year. A lovely choice for the rock garden or for growing in pans is *C. sieberi*. The form 'Hubert Edelsten' is purple and white; 'Violet Queen' is deep mauve. A bright yellow alternative is *C. ancyrensis* 'Golden Bunch'. For naturalizing, plant *C. tommasinianus*.

LARGE-FLOWERED DUTCH CROCUSES
The large-flowered hybrid crocuses may lack the subtle colouring and form of the species crocuses but their substance and bold colouring make them valuable bulbs for planting in borders or naturalizing in grass to flower in mid-spring. Among many named forms, the following have long been popular: 'Dutch Yellow' ('Large Yellow'), earlier than most and bright yellow; 'Joan of Arc', white; 'Pickwick', mauve and 'Remembrance', violet-purple.

Crocus chrysanthus 'Cream Beauty'.

A *Crocus tommasinianus* variety.

Cyclamen

HARDY SPECIES Hardy cyclamen must rank among the most desirable of dwarf garden plants for shady positions in the rock garden or for naturalizing under trees or shrubs. The charm of their flowers, pink or magenta and with albino forms also available, is often matched by the beauty of marbled foliage. The most widely available autumn-flowering species is *C. hederifolium (C. neapolitanum)*, which grows to 15cm (6in) and is exceptionally free-flowering and long-lived. Among other species, *C. purpurascens (C. europaeum)* flowers in autumn, *C. coum* in winter and early spring and *C. repandum* in late spring.

FLORISTS' CYCLAMEN In early winter the florists' cyclamen are among the most popular of houseplants. Selected forms of the species *C. persicum* have given rise to strains with large flowers, some scented. The range of colours includes white, pink, salmon and purple; some have ruffled petals and many, particularly those of the 'Rex' strain, have beautifully silvered leaves.

Dierama

(Wandflower) The name 'wandflower' refers to the slender stems that arch over to carry the hanging flowers of these graceful South African plants. A more fanciful name is angel's fishing rod. The most commonly grown species is *D. pulcherrimum*, which grows to about 1.5m (5ft) in height. Flowers are borne in late summer; plants need sun, warmth and adequate moisture.

In early winter the florists' cyclamen are popular as houseplants.

The winter aconite, *Eranthis × tubergenii*, blooms in mid-winter.

Erythronium revolutum 'White Beauty'.

Eranthis
(Winter aconite) This lives up to its name by coming into flower from mid- to late winter, and has yellow, globular flowers set off by a green ruff, up to 10cm (4in) high. It associates well with other winter-flowering bulbs, particularly when naturalized under shrubs. The easiest and most widely grown species is *E. hyemalis*. A hybrid, *E. × tubergenii*, generally sold as the named form 'Guinea Gold', has a larger flower and the leaves are tinged bronze.

Erythronium
(Dog's-tooth violet) The erythroniums are among the most useful and beautiful small hardy bulbs for planting in shady positions under deciduous trees. The graceful reflexed flowers, 15–25cm (6–10in) high, are borne in mid- to late spring. The dog's-tooth violet *(E. dens-canis)*, the sole European species, has beautifully marbled leaves. The cultivated forms, which range in colour from white to purple, include: 'Lilac Wonder', 'Rose Beauty' and 'White Splendour'. Hybrids of the American species include 'Pagoda', which has sunny yellow flowers, and 'White Beauty'.

Large-flowered freesia hybrids.

Fritillaria imperialis 'Lutea'.

Freesia

LARGE-FLOWERED FREESIA HYBRIDS
The exquisitely scented freesias *(F. × kewensis)* that are so valued in winter are hybrids of South African species. The sprays of flowers in a wide range of colours on stems up to 60cm (2ft) tall can be produced by growing the bulbs indoors. Alternatively, treated bulbs, now available from some nurserymen, can be planted outdoors in late spring for flowering in summer.

Fritillaria

(Fritillary) One fritillary, the crown imperial *(F. imperialis)* has for centuries been valued as a spring-flowering bulb of imposing scale. The brick-red flowers hang in a cluster beneath a whorl of leaves at the head of a stem up to 1.2m (4ft) tall. Variations in colour include 'Lutea', lemon yellow, and 'Rubra', red. The snake's-head fritillary *(F. meleagris)* is among the best bulbs for naturalizing in moist positions.

Fritillaria meleagris **likes moisture.**

Galanthus

(Snowdrop) The snowdrops, which flower at the end of winter, are excellent bulbs for naturalizing under deciduous trees and for growing in clumps in the rockery. All the species are remarkably consistent in appearance, producing the nodding white flowers on stems 12–20cm (5–8in) high. The common snowdrop *(G. nivalis)* is as beautiful as any. 'Atkinsii' is particularly vigorous and large-flowered. Later-flowering *G. elwesii* is distinguished by its broad, greyish leaves.

Galtonia

(Summer hyacinth) In its native South Africa, where it is a plant of mountain areas, *G. candicans* is sometimes known as the berg lily. As many as twenty-five creamy flowers are borne on tall stems, up to 1.2m (4ft) high, in mid- to late summer. They look very attractive in a sunny position among shrubs.

Galanthus or snowdrops are ideal for naturalizing under deciduous trees.

The large-flowered gladioli are available in a wide range of colours.

Gladiolus

GLADIOLUS SPECIES The species are much less showy than the widely grown hybrids but include plants of great distinction. One of the most beautiful is *G. callianthus* (still often listed under the name *Acidanthera bicolor*). It produces stems up to 90cm (3ft) high, bearing elegant, sweetly scented flowers that are pure white, blotched purple at the throat. It is grown in the same way as the hybrid gladioli. *G. byzantinus* is hardy so need not be lifted.

LARGE-FLOWERED HYBRID GLADIOLI The modern, large-flowered, hybrid gladioli rank among the most spectacular summer-flowering bulbous plants. The handsome spikes of funnel-shaped flowers, to 1.2m (4ft) high and available in a very wide range of colours, make an attractive feature in the border or are excellent for cutting. The choice of named forms will depend on one's colour preferences. The Primulinus hybrids are similar but have less densely packed and smaller hooded florets.

MINIATURE HYBRID GLADIOLI The neat shape of the miniature gladioli makes them an attractive alternative to the massive, large-flowered hybrids, which they match in range of colour. The flower spikes grow to a height of 45–90cm (1½-3ft). The butterfly hybrids, a strain of the miniatures, are attractively marked and the petals have an unusual wavy edge.

Hippeastrum

(Amaryllis) The use of the common name amaryllis for these spectacular indoor plants unfortunately confuses them with the true amaryllis. Most of the hippeastrums available are hybrids and are sold according to flower colour. By maintaining a temperature of not less than 15°C (60°F) they can be made to bloom in mid-winter. The flower stems grow to 45cm (1½ft) bearing three or four huge, trumpet-shaped flowers ranging in colour from white to deep red.

Butterfly gladioli – attractively marked.

Hippeastrums can be made to bloom in mid-winter given adequate warmth.

Large-flowered hyacinths are richly scented. Grow indoors or outside.

Hyacinthoides
(Bluebell) The common English bluebell *(H. non-scripta)* is so free-spreading that it can be a nuisance other than in a semi-wild garden or in woodland but in these positions it is one of the glories of late spring. There are white and pink forms as well as blue. All grow to about 35cm (14in). The Spanish bluebell *(H. hispanica)* is a similarly robust and free-flowering plant for the wild garden. (Both of these species are still sometimes to be found listed under *Endymion* or *Scilla*.)

Hyacinthus
LARGE-FLOWERED HYACINTHS The large-flowered and richly scented hyacinths, which have been developed from *H. orientalis*, are among the best of the bulbs for forcing and for this specially prepared bulbs should be bought. Planted outdoors in bedding schemes or in containers, such as windowboxes, unprepared bulbs come into flower in mid-spring. All grow to about 20cm (8in) and the colour range includes white, blue, pink, red and yellow.

***Ipheion uniflorum*, blooms early spring.**

Ipheion
Only one species, *I. uniflorum* (which has sometimes been listed under *Brodiaea, Milla* or *Triteleia*), is in general cultivation. It is an easy plant in a sunny well-drained position, the pale blue star-shaped flowers being borne on stems about 15cm (6in) high over a long period in early spring. 'Wisley Blue' is a large-flowered form of good colour.

Iris

DWARF IRIS SPECIES Despite their delicate appearance, the dwarf irises, generally not more than 15cm (6in) high, stand up remarkably well to the worst weather of late winter and early spring and are among the choicest of the early bulbs. The best known is *I. reticulata*, which is deep blue with gold on the falls. Named forms of various colouring include 'Cantab', 'Clairette', 'Harmony', 'Joyce' and 'J.S. Dijt'. Among other species worth seeking out is the yellow *I. danfordiae* and the brilliant blue *I. histrioides 'Major'*.

Dutch irises are hardy hybrids.

DUTCH IRIS The hardy hybrid irises derived from *I. tingitana* and *I. xiphium* are useful border plants and excellent for cutting. The stems are about 75cm (2½ft) high and the colour range includes white, yellow and blue. They are increasingly sold as mixtures rather than as named varieties. The Spanish irises, derived from *I. xiphium*, flower a few weeks earlier and the more solid English irises, forms and hybrids of *I. xiphioides*, are in flower in mid- to late summer.

Leucojum

(Snowflake) The snowflakes are excellent plants for naturalizing, and are reasonably tolerant of shade. Despite its name, the summer snowflake *(L. aestivum)* flowers in late spring, growing to 60cm (2ft) and bearing nodding white flowers tipped green. 'Gravetye Giant' is a particularly good form. The spring snowflake *(L. vernum)* and the autumn snowflake *(L autumnale)* are smaller plants and the flowers of the latter are tinged pink.

Iris reticulata **varieties and the yellow** *Iris danfordiae*.

Lilium

LILY SPECIES There are now so many hybrid lilies available that the species can be overlooked in spite of their merits and beauty. The regal lily *(L. regale)* is an easy plant worth a place in any collection. The white funnel-shaped flowers, shaded purple on the outside and richly scented, are produced in clusters on stems up to 1.8m (6ft) high in midsummer. Other valuable species include *L. auratum, L. candidum, L. davidii, L. henryi, L. martagon* and *L. speciosum.*

MID-CENTURY HYBRID LILIES This group contains a number of hybrids of exceptional quality having wide, speckled flowers in a range of colours from lemon to deep red. 'Enchantment' is a very fine example with large cup-shaped flowers of an intense orange-red. It is suitable for forcing or growing outdoors, where it will flower in early summer. Other noteworthy varieties are 'Cinnabar', with bright red flowers, and 'Destiny', with yellow flowers.

TRUMPET LILY HYBRIDS Among the most impressive of the hybrid lilies are those with trumpet-shaped flowers that have been derived from Asiatic species. Some of the best belong to the Aurelian hybrids, one of which is 'African Queen'. This stem-rooting variety grows to 1.5m (5ft) and produces, in the second half of summer, a pyramid of yellow-orange flowers. 'Black Dragon', an Olympic hybrid, and the Pink Perfection strain are other examples of some of the most magnificent flowering bulbs.

TURK'S CAP HYBRID LILIES A number of hybrid lilies have elegant recurved petals in the style of *L. martagon.* One of the loveliest is 'Marhan', which in early summer produces stems bearing eight or more orange flowers spotted red. The Bellingham, Fiesta and Harlequin hybrids also have flowers of turk's-cap form.

ABOVE *Lilium regale* or regal lily.

LEFT Mid-century hybrid 'Destiny'.

Muscari

(Grape hyacinth) Some of the grape hyacinths, including *M. neglectum*, can be too vigorous and leafy to warrant cultivation but *M. armeniacum* is an easy and desirable bulb flowering in mid-spring, particularly useful for naturalizing among shrubs. The bright blue flowers borne on stems up to 20cm (8in) high, have a fine white rim. 'Heavenly Blue' is intense in colour, 'Cantab' paler. There is also a double form, 'Blue Spike'.

Hoop petticoat *Narcissus bulbocodium*.

***Muscari armeniacum* or grape hyacinth.**

Narcissus

DWARF NARCISSUS SPECIES Of the dwarf species one of the loveliest and most unusual is the little hoop petticoat narcissus *(N. bulbocodium)*. It gets its name from the distinctive funnel-shaped trumpet, which dominates the small petals, on stems rarely more than 15cm (6in) high. The colour is generally golden yellow but there are forms of paler and deeper colour. It is ideal for a moist position in the rock garden or for naturalizing in thin grass.

ANGEL'S TEARS NARCISSUS Some of the most refined of the miniature narcissus hybrids have been derived from the angel's tears narcissus *(N. triandrus)* which itself is a very desirable plant. 'Thalia' is a lovely variety, growing to about 40cm (16in) and bearing three or more hanging white flowers per stem. Others showing the family characteristics are: 'April Tears' and 'Liberty Bells', both yellow, and 'Silver Chimes', white. All are lovely in the rock garden and can also be naturalized satisfactorily.

BUNCH-FLOWERED NARCISSI The best-known of the bunch-flowered narcissi is 'Paper White', a variety of the tazetta narcissus *(N. tazetta)*. It is generally too tender to grow outdoors but because it is early flowering it makes an ideal bulb for the house in winter. Up to ten pure white flowers, deliciously scented, are borne on stems up to 45cm (1½ft) high. Hardy tazetta hybrids include 'Geranium', white with orange cup, and two good doubles, 'Cheerfulness', creamy yellow, and 'Yellow Cheerfulness'.

CYCLAMINEUS HYBRID DAFFODILS The dwarf *N. cyclamineus*, itself a beautiful daffodil for moist positions, is a parent of a group of early-flowering trumpet daffodils that are shorter growing than most garden daffodils and have elegant flowers with recurved petals. 'Jack Snipe', which has a creamy perianth and yellow trumpet, is a fine example that grows to about 20cm (8in). Other all yellow varieties are 'February Gold', 'Peeping Tom' and 'Tête-à-Tête' (two or more flowers per stem).

JONQUILS The jonquils, which have several flowers to a stem, are the most sweetly scented of all the narcissi, this characteristic being derived from the common parent of the modern hybrids, *N. jonquilla*. 'Baby Moon' is a short-growing variety, reaching 20cm (8in) and bearing numerous stems of soft yellow flowers in mid-spring. Larger-growing varieties include: 'Bobbysoxer', yellow with an orange cup; 'Suzy', also yellow and orange; and 'Trevithian', which is pale yellow.

Tazetta narcissus 'Yellow Cheerfulness'.

Tazetta narcissus 'Geranium' is well known and easily grown.

Cyclamineus hybrid daffodil 'Peeping Tom' flowers early in the season.

LARGE-CUPPED DAFFODILS This large group of daffodils of garden origin includes one of the best of all daffodil varieties, 'Carlton', which flowers in early spring and is suitable for forcing as well as growing outdoors, has a particularly large cup and is a clear strong yellow. Other large-cupped varieties include: 'Duke of Windsor', white perianth and yellow cup; 'Ice Follies', white perianth and cream cup; and 'Red Rascal', a colourful variety with a yellow perianth and orange cup.

TRUMPET DAFFODILS Among the boldest of the daffodils are the large trumpet hybrids. The uniformly deep yellow 'Golden Harvest' is a prolific and reliable example of the type but other colour combinations are also available. 'Mount Hood', for instance, is almost pure white, 'Magnet' has a yellow trumpet and white perianth, while 'Passionale' has a pinkish trumpet and white perianth. All grow to about 45cm (1½ft) and flower early to mid-spring.

SMALL-CUPPED DAFFODILS The small-cupped daffodils with a single flower to a stem have an elegance that some of the bolder varieties lack. 'Edward Buxton' is a lovely example, having a pale yellow perianth and a vivid orange cup. Other examples include: 'Barrett Browning', white perianth and orange cup; 'Birma', yellow perianth and orange cup; and 'La Riante', white perianth and deep orange cup. The variety 'Actaea' of the poet's narcissus *(N. poeticus)* is a small-cupped daffodil of exceptional refinement.

Nerine
Given a warm sheltered position, *N. bowdenii*, a reasonably hardy species of a group of bulbs coming mainly from southern Africa, will produce a splendid display of pink flowers in autumn. Stiff stems, up to 60cm (2ft) high, carry heads of up to ten flowers, the petals of which recurve and have a slightly waved edge. They are excellent for cutting. 'Fenwick's Variety' is a large-flowered and vigorous form.

Ornithogalum
(Star of Bethlehem) Many of the ornithogalums have starry white flowers with a greenish stripe. The most common, *O. umbellatum*, spreads too quickly to be recommended but *O. nutans* is a lovely plant for naturalizing at the base of hedges and under shrubs. It grows to 45cm (1½ft), producing its delicate stems of drooping flowers in the late spring.

Scilla
(Squill) In early spring the brilliant blue of *S. sibirica* is one of the delights of the rock garden. Although only growing to about 15cm (6in), it can be satisfactorily naturalized in short grass. 'Spring Beauty' is a form of exceptionally intense colouring. A smaller species, flowering as early as mid-winter, is *S. tubergeniana*, which has pale blue flowers.

Sternbergia
The sternbergias provide a welcome splash of brilliant yellow when their crocus-like flowers open in autumn. The most readily available species, *S. lutea,* which stands about 15cm (6in) high, will flower freely if left undisturbed in a sunny well-drained position where it can get a good baking in the summer.

Tigridia pavonia is half-hardy.

Ornithogalum umbellatum is vigorous.

Tigridia
(Tiger flower) The half-hardy tiger flowers *(T. pavonia)* are brilliantly coloured, generally in shades of yellow and scarlet. The flower stems grow to 60cm (2ft) and each flower consists of three large, usually unmarked, petals and a base with three tiny petals vividly spotted crimson brown. Individual flowers last only a day but each corm produces six or more so that, if you plant them in succession, a good display can be maintained for several weeks in summer.

Tulipa

Tulip species. Quite different in scale to the hybrid tulips is the graceful lady tulip *(T. clusiana)*, a species that has long been in cultivation and which is worth a sunny well-drained spot in any rock garden. The slender stems, up to 30cm (1ft), bear white flowers that are deep pink on the outside in mid-spring. Other good tulip species include *T. chrysantha, T. praestans* and *T. tarda.*

DARWIN TULIPS The Darwin tulips are popular for bedding schemes in late spring. They grow to 60cm (2ft) and the flowers are somewhat rounded in shape. The rose-pink 'Clara Butt' has long been one of the most popular varieties. Others to choose from include: 'Queen of Night', dark purple; 'Sweet Harmony', yellow; and 'Paul Richter', which is a distinctive shade of red.

DARWIN HYBRID TULIPS The magnificent tall-growing tulips of this group, most grow to 60cm (2ft) at least, are the result of crossing the Darwin tulips with *T. fosteriana.* They flower in late spring, shortly before the Darwin tulips, their height allowing for underplanting in bedding schemes. 'Apeldorn', which has glossy scarlet flowers with a black yellow-edged base, is one of the best. The colour range includes: 'Elizabeth Arden', salmon pink; 'Holland's Glory', orange red; and 'Olympic Flame', yellow with red feathering.

DOUBLE EARLY TULIPS This strain of tulips produces double paeony-like flowers in mid-spring on stout stems that are rarely more than 30cm (1ft) high. They are popular for forcing and suitable, too, for bedding. 'Orange Nassau', which is a rich orange-red, is one of the best. Others include 'Maréchal Niel', yellow; 'Peach Blossom', pink; and 'Schoonoord', white.

FOSTERIANA HYBRID TULIPS This group of tulips, generally 30–45cm (1–1½ft) high, derived from *T. fosteriana*, includes some vividly coloured varieties that are excellent early-flowering border plants. The pure white 'Purissima' (sometimes known as 'White Emperor') is an outstanding example. Others include: 'Candela', yellow; 'Cantata', red; and 'Orange Emperor', orange.

Double early tulip 'Orange Nassau'.

Darwin tulip, for spring bedding.

45

GREIGII HYBRID TULIPS The dwarf hybrid tulips derived from *T. greigii* include some of the best varieties for the rock garden, for growing in window boxes and for planting in clumps to give a brilliant effect in borders. Most grow to about 25cm (10in), flower in mid-spring and have handsomely streaked or mottled leaves. The vivid scarlet 'Red Riding Hood' deserves its popularity. Among other good varieties are: 'Cape Cod', yellow and apricot; 'Dreamboat', apricot; and 'Plaisir', cream and vermilion.

LILY-FLOWERED TULIPS This is a particularly elegant strain of garden tulip with long pointed petals that curve back. They are generally 50cm (20in) or more in height and flower in late spring. In bedding schemes they create a lighter effect than some of the other garden tulips. 'Queen of Sheba' is a splendid variety that has rusty red flowers edged with orange. Other good varieties are: 'China Pink', pink; 'West Point', yellow; and 'White Triumphator', white for a cool contrast.

REMBRANDT TULIPS As can be seen from many old paintings, striped and feathered tulips were once highly valued by Dutch breeders. The 'breaking' is caused by viruses so that these tulips are not as vigorous as other varieties. They are, however, very attractive as cut flowers. Usually, they are now available only as mixtures. The same is true of the parrot tulips, which have fringed and cut petals.

Lily-flowered tulip 'White Triumphator'.

Tulipa greigii '**Cape Cod', ideal for rock gardens and window boxes.**

A mixture of waterlily tulips, which flower in early spring.

SINGLE EARLY TULIPS These hardy tulips flower outdoors in mid-spring, just as the species and their varieties are finishing. They are also frequently forced for flowering indoors. They are sturdy plants, 30–38cm (12–15in) high. The golden orange 'General de Wet' (sometimes listed as 'De Wet') is one of the best. Other varieties of some distinction include 'Bellona', yellow; 'Couleur Cardinal', red to purple; and 'Diana', another attractive white variety.

TRIUMPH HYBRID TULIPS The varieties belonging to this group flower in mid-spring – they are the result of crosses between the single early tulips and late-flowering varieties – so that they are often used in schemes where beds need to be cleared early for new planting. They are sturdy plants, growing to about 50cm (20in). 'Garden Party', with pink and white flowers, is a very striking example. Other varieties include: 'Apricot Beauty', salmon; 'Kansas', white; and 'Reforma', yellow.

WATERLILY TULIPS A range of brilliantly coloured and generally dwarf tulips has been developed from the waterlily tulip (T. kaufmanniana). They flower in early spring and are excellent for the rock garden or border. 'Heart's Delight' is a good example. The outside of the flower is carmine red with a pale edge and the inside is white with a yellow base. It grows to about 25cm (10in) and the leaves are beautifully marked with purplish streaks. Other varieties include: 'Shakespeare', apricot; 'Stresa', yellow and orange; and 'The First', white.

INDEX AND ACKNOWLEDGEMENTS

Picture Credits

Pat Brindley: 1,20,32,33(b),34(tl),35,37(b),38(t,b),39(t),40(br),41(l),
  42(t,b),44(t),45(bl,br),47.
Lyn & Derek Gould: 12,26/7,28(t,b).
John Glover: 7(b).
S & O Mathews: 14(b).
Harry Smith Horticultural Photographic Collection: 4/5,9(t),13(t),14(t),18,
  31(l),34(tr),36,37(t),39(b),44(b),46(t,b).
Michael Warren: 6,7(t),8,9(b),13(b),15,21,22,23(t,b),29,30,31(r),33(t),34(b),
  40(bl),41(r),43.

Artwork by Simon Roulstone

48